T0199074

GOD HATES DARKNESS

Light Has Dominion Over Darkness

S A R A H   O D U N L A M I

AuthorHouse™ UK
1663 Liberty Drive
Bloomington, IN 47403 USA
www.authorhouse.co.uk
Phone: UK TFN: 0800 0148641 (Toll Free inside the UK)
UK Local: 02036 956322 (+44 20 3695 6322 from outside the UK)

Because of the dynamic nature of the Internet, any web addresses or links contained in this book may have changed since publication and may no longer be valid. The views expressed in this work are solely those of the author and do not necessarily reflect the views of the publisher, and the publisher hereby disclaims any responsibility for them.

Any people depicted in stock imagery provided by Getty Images are models, and such images are being used for illustrative purposes only. Certain stock imagery © Getty Images.

This book is printed on acid-free paper.

Scriptures marked KJV are taken from the KING JAMES VERSION (KJV): KING JAMES VERSION, public domain.

ISBN: 978-1-7283-5388-3 (sc)
978-1-7283-5387-6 (e)

Print information available on the last page.

Published by AuthorHouse 06/04/2020

authorHOUSE

The LORD God made everything in the whole world. Including the Light and Darkness. But Darkness became an obstacle to the works of God. So, the LORD God decided to destroy Darkness. Darkness wanted to dominate the Light but it could not, because the Light is powerful than it. The Light is the winner. The Light has dominion over Darkness.

ACKNOWLEDGEMENT

I would like to sincerely appreciate my wonderful husband Mr. Ishola Tirimisiyu Odunlami (brother Thimothy) for his participation in making sure that all goes well with the writing of this book by prayer and supplication to God.

I also thank God for using my children Mojishola Odunlami, Matthew Odunlami and Miracle Odunlami to give useful ideas for the success of this book.

I would also like to use this opportunity to appreciate Pastor Yinka Babajinde, Pastor Emmanuel Aboluwade and Pastor Morenikeji Margaret Gbenga for being the major contributors to my spiritual growth. Also, Dr. Yetunde Adesanya, as a best friend that was also there for me.

Of course how can I forget God Almighty who supplied me with all the necessary information and wisdom that I needed. God I thank you so much in the name of our Lord Jesus Christ.

AiM TO:

- Help children all over the world get closer to God.

- Let children know that God cannot stay where darkness is.

- Let children know that everything is made by someone called God.

- Make sure that children learn how to depend on God.

- Teach children the basic ideas about the creation.

- Help children to find the word of God pleasant to read.

- Let children know that God has the power to make decisions over everything he had made.

One day, The LORD God realised that darkness is causing trouble.

Darkness is one of the things that the
LORD God made with his hands.

God is thinking about how to destroy darkness.

The LORD God loves everything he had made but he hates
darkness so much. So he decided to get rid of darkness.

The LORD God became very angry about darkness.

No, no, no!

I will not allow darkness
to ruin my works.

I have to find a solution quickly.

I cannot take this anymore.

I need to take action
before it is too late.

The LORD God is not happy because of the presence of darkness.

The LORD GOD is now looking for the
Light everywhere to destroy darkness.

Darkness is in big trouble now because
The Light is about to destroy it.

The LORD God finally had an idea.
The Light is getting ready to destroy darkness.

Darkness is in trouble with The Light.

The Light is on a special mission.
The Light is about to destroy darkness.
The Light and darkness are having a talk.

The Light is very stronger than darkness.

Finally, he was very stubborn. No wonder,
God wanted me to get rid of him.

He was even talking back at me.

He does not know that I am God's favourite one.

At least I have destroyed him.
Mission accomplished!

The Light is now going to give account to God.

The LORD God is about to find out if the job is done.

God gave dominion to the Light.
Now, the Light can rule over darkness forever.

The Light is very happy to be the winner.

The End

QUESTIONS:

Ask your child to tell you the name of the author of this book?

Ask your child to tell you the names of the three characters of this book?

Ask your child to tell you whose name is All Powerful in this book?

Ask your child to tell you the hero inside this book?

Ask your child to tell you what the LORD God gave the Light? And why?

Ask your child to tell you where darkness is now?

Ask your child how he/she felt after reading the book?

Finally, ask your child to draw one of the characters of this book?

ABOUT THE AUTHOR

My name is Sarah Odunlami. But I am officially known as Sadia Odunlami. I am an Evangelist Of God. Called to preach the good News of our Lord Jesus to all nations of the World. My commission is to spread out the word God all over the World. I gave my life to Jesus in the year 2015. My experience as a Christian is unexplainable. To me, Christianity is more than a religion. I picture Christianity as an ability to develop close relationship with God through his words.

I am happily married with three beautiful children.

I hold a Second Class degree in Biopharmaceutical/ Pharmaceutical Science from Dundalk Institute of Technology, Ireland Republic.

Address: 2 Taylor Place, Glasgow, G40NY.

Tel: +44-7984608590.

ALL RiGHTS RESERVE:

Printed in the United States
By Bookmasters